T0380905

My little masterpiece

by

Bienvenido Flores

To order additional copies of this book, contact:
Xlibris
1-800-455-039
www.xlibris.com.au
Orders@Xlibris.com.au

Bio

This book was inspired by sons words, "Dad please write a book". Well here you have it, Adolfo Flores-Maestre. I hope it inspires you and who ever reads it.

When the inspiration

hits you
light up
your

imagination.

Cuando

la inspiracion

te toca

enciende tu

imaginacion.

Make it easy
in the quest

lies

your Magic.

Haz lo facil

en la conquista

se esconde

la magia.

If you don't
push yourself
you will never know
on what you have
missed out.

Si no te esfuerzas nunca sabras lo Que en realidad te habras perdido.

Every day gives you **the best** and just one great **idea** will give you the rest.

Cada dia te da lo mas
pero una gran
idea
te dara
lo demas.

" If your dream
is big
just wait

and see it

come
to you."

"Si tu sueño es

inmenso

solo espera y veras

como un dia

Èste té

llegara."

Control the moment
release
your Talent.

Controla
el momento,
y envuelve este
con tu talento.

You can either

wait or chase

or be patient

and observe

how the magic

touches you.

Puedes esperar
o volar,
o ser paciente
y observar
como la magia
te toca.

What is Passion?

Passion is that which **drives you** to limitless faith. Illuminating the path **to your** dreams.

Que es la pasíon?
La pasión es aquello
que te conlleva
a disponer y
a tener una fè
sin limites.
Iluminando
el camino
de tus sueños.

Remember
that you possess
a great gift

it's called expression.
don't forget
to use it.

Recuerda

Que posees un gran

regalo

este se llama expresion,

no te olvides

de usarlo.

Step it up

take another breath

and make today

your

best

day.

Un paso
hacia delante
respira hondo
y haz
de este dia
tu mayor dia.

The inspiration usually comes to those who are willing to share it.

La inspiracion suele llegarte cuando estas dispuesto a compartir está.

TODAY IS GREY
AND WINDY

BUT THE SKIES WHERE BRIGTH

AND INTUITIVELY BLUE

FOR ME
IT'S SO
POWERFUL AND ITS CALLED
FRIENDSHIP.

HOY ES GRIS
Y HACE VIENTO
PERO LOS CIELOS ESTAN
RESPLANDECIENTES
Y INTUITIVAMENTE AZULES
PARA MI.
ESTO ES TAN PODEROSO
Y SE LLAMA
AMISTAD.

Under every story of Success there is a timetable attached to it.

Bajo cualquier historia de exito hay una programacion sujeta a esta.

Printed in the United States
By Bookmasters